Daniel and the Puppet Master

Written by Janine Scott

Illustrated by Chantal de Sousa

Daniel and his dad were excited to finally be in Malaysia. They had been planning this trip for more than a year.

They were going to meet Daniel's pen pal, Jalak, for the first time.

It had been an hour's drive, a two-hour wait at the airport and then an eight-hour flight to get to Malaysia. They were now travelling on a bus that would take them to Jalak's village.

At first, the view outside looked like home.

There were busy roads, big buildings and people everywhere.

After they had left the city, things looked different. There were forests, hills and rivers. The bus bumped along the dirt roads.

Daniel and his dad found Jalak's village on their map.

"It won't be long now," said Dad.

In the distance, Daniel could see a boy and his mum at the bus stop, waving.

"I think that's Jalak!" Daniel said excitedly. "He looks just like his photo."

After waiting for the bus to stop, Daniel raced to greet his pen pal.

Daniel's dad got off the bus and walked over to Jalak's mum.

“It is very nice to meet you,” said Daniel’s dad. “Thank you for inviting us to stay.”

“We are pleased you are here,” said Jalak’s mum. “Our village is nearby. We can walk there.”

Jalak and Daniel walked together.

Jalak was telling Daniel about the animals that live in the forest. He pointed to a beautiful green lizard on a tree branch.

“Do you think I’ll see some monkeys while I’m here?” asked Daniel. “They’re my favourite animal.”

“Of course,” replied Jalak. “Monkeys live near our village. They always visit us.”

The walk to the village was longer than Daniel had thought it would be.

Jalak and Daniel passed some rice fields. There were people in the fields planting rice.

"Our village grows lots of rice," explained Jalak. "Rice is Malaysia's main food crop."

“What is that boy doing over there?” asked Daniel.

“He is fishing,” said Jalak. “Small fish live in the flooded rice fields. The fish are very tasty.”

Before long, they arrived at the village. Jalak took Daniel and his dad on a tour.

"Why are all the houses on stilts?" asked Daniel.

"The village is by a river," explained Jalak. "If the river floods, the house will stay dry. The stilts also let air go under the house. That helps keep the house cool."

“That one is my house,” Jalak pointed to one of the houses.

Daniel’s dad went inside for a rest.

Jalak’s grandfather was sitting outside. He was holding a shadow puppet and a paintbrush.

“Grandfather,” said Jalak. “This is my friend Daniel.”

“Hello, Daniel,” said Grandfather. “Welcome to our village.”

“Thank you,” said Daniel. “It’s very nice to meet you. What are you holding?”

“I have made a shadow puppet,” said Grandfather. “I was about to paint it. Different colours mean different things. Red means anger. Warrior puppets often have red faces.”

“Grandfather is a puppet master,” explained Jalak. “He makes shadow puppets and puts on shadow puppet shows. Puppet shows are popular in Malaysian culture. They have been around for hundreds of years. It is one way we pass down our folk tales.”

“Come to my workshop,” said Grandfather. “I can show you how to make a puppet.”

“Grandfather makes puppets with leather,” explained Jalak. “His father taught him. Now Grandfather teaches other people his skills.”

“What kind of puppet would you like to make?” Jalak asked Daniel.

Daniel thought carefully for a moment. “I want to make a monkey puppet!”

Grandfather got out his cutting tool. He cut a monkey puppet out of leather.

Daniel’s dad helped by cutting patterns in the leather. Then Daniel painted the puppet.

Daniel gazed at his monkey puppet. He was very proud of it.

"We put on shadow puppet shows on special occasions," said Jalak. "There will be one tomorrow night."

“Grandfather,” said Jalak. “Could Daniel help with the puppet show?”

“I’d love to!” said Daniel excitedly. “If it’s okay?”

Grandfather nodded slowly. “Daniel, you are a special guest of this village. I would be honoured if you would help. But there is no time to waste. Your monkey puppet will be one of the characters in the show!”

“Wow!” said Daniel, jumping up in excitement. “I promise to work hard. I can’t wait to be in a real shadow puppet show!”

On the night of the show, everyone in the village sat in front of a white cloth screen.

It was dark all around.

Suddenly, a light shone from behind the screen. Some musicians began to play their drums and gongs.

One shadow puppet came on the screen. Then Daniel's monkey puppet appeared.

Grandfather began to tell a story about the two puppets.

Daniel made his puppet dance and move to the music. He remembered all the actions that Grandfather had taught him that day.

As the show came to an end, the musicians ended their song.

The light went out from behind the screen.

The audience began to clap, getting louder and louder.

Grandfather stepped out from the behind the screen, bringing Daniel with him.

Daniel looked for his dad in the crowd. He was standing next to Jalak and Jalak's mum. They were all smiling and clapping madly.

Daniel waved back. He would never forget his first trip to Malaysia.